How Are Cars Made and Sold?

Bridey Heing

Cavendish Square

New York

Published in 2020 by Cavendish Square Publishing, LLC
243 5th Avenue, Suite 136, New York, NY 10016

Copyright © 2020 by Cavendish Square Publishing, LLC

First Edition

Library of Congress Cataloging-in-Publication Data

Names: Heing, Bridey, author.
Title: How are cars made and sold? / Bridey Heing.
Description: First edition. | New York, NY : Cavendish Square Publishing, LLC, 2020. |
Series: Where do goods come from? |
Includes bibliographical references and index. | Audience: Grades 2 to 5.
Identifiers: LCCN 2019019736 (print) | LCCN 2019020854 (ebook) | ISBN
9781502650467 (library bound : alk. paper) | ISBN 9781502650443 (pbk. :
alk. paper) | ISBN 9781502650450 (6 pack : alk. paper)
Subjects: LCSH: Automobiles--History--Juvenile literature.|
Automobile industry and trade--United States--History--Juvenile literature.
Classification: LCC TL147 .H455 2020 (print) | LCC TL147 (ebook) |
DDC 629.222--dc23
LC record available at https://lccn.loc.gov/2019019736
LC ebook record available at https://lccn.loc.gov/2019020854

Editor: Caitlyn Miller
Copy Editor: Denise Larrabee
Associate Art Director: Alan Sliwinski
Designer: Christina Shults
Production Coordinator: Karol Szymczuk
Photo Research: J8 Media

The photographs in this book are used by permission and through the courtesy of:
Cover Nataliya Hora/Shutterstock.com; pp. 5, 13 Monty Rakusen/Cultura/Getty Images; p. 6 Aleksandr
Kondratov/Shutterstock.com; p. 8 hadynyah/E+/Getty Images; p. 9 Nick-Roberts/Shutterstock.com;
p. 11 Alexander Chizhenok/Shutterstock.com; p. 14 Jenson/
Shutterstock.com; p. 19 canaran/iStock/Getty Images; p. 21 Anadolu Agency/Getty Images; p. 22
andresr/E+/Getty Images; p. 27 Benoist/Shutterstock.com; p. 28 Joseph Sohm/Shutterstock.com.

Printed in the United States of America

Table of Contents

Chapter 1

Sourcing Cars

A lot of people drive or ride in a car every day. Almost 90 percent of households in the United States own a car. That's more than 260 million cars! Every car is made of around 30,000 parts. Most parts are made from steel, aluminum, plastic, rubber, and glass.

What a Car Is Made Of

Steel is one of a car's most important materials. Steel is a metal. It is used for the **chassis** of the car. The chassis is what the rest of the car is built on.

Steel is a metal used to make cars. It's shown here in rolls.

Aluminum is used to make cars too. Aluminum is a metal, but it is not heavy. The **body** of a car is

DID YOU KNOW?

The first vehicle resembling a car was made in 1769. It was made by Nicolas-Joseph Cugnot. It was made of metal and wood. It ran on steam.

Parts inside of a car and in the engine are made of plastic.

usually made of aluminum. That means aluminum is used to make the doors, the hood, and more.

Car parts are also made of plastic. Plastic is used for many parts of a car. It is used for the steering wheel and the seat belts. It is also used for parts in the engine.

Tires are made of rubber. Rubber is used in car engines as well. It helps cars last longer.

Car windows are made of glass. Glass in cars is strong. It needs to be hard to break! This helps keep us safe.

Where Do Materials Come From?

The materials cars are made of come from around the world. Companies that make car parts need raw materials from lots of countries. Raw materials are turned into glass, steel, and more.

Rubber is made from **latex**. Latex comes from rubber trees. Rubber trees grow in places like South America and Asia. Steel is made from iron. Some

DID YOU KNOW?

Sand can be used to make glass. It is shipped by train and truck. Large amounts of sand can be very heavy. Trucks have to be careful when moving it because it can damage the road.

Rubber is made from latex. Latex is harvested from trees.

iron is mined in the United States, Canada, and Brazil. Oil is used to make plastic. Oil comes from places like Texas, Alaska, and the Middle East.

Saving the Environment

Getting all the materials to make a car can be hard on the planet. Mining iron can pollute the

Oil companies drill in different places. These oil platforms are in Texas.

air and water. Oil drilling can harm the soil and water. Farming rubber can harm the soil too. Car companies can try to help the planet. They can use new materials that don't harm nature. They can also find safe ways to get what they need. For example, some companies only buy rubber that is grown in ways that don't pollute soil or harm workers.

Chapter 2

Making Cars

Cars are made around the world. Different countries make different cars. This happens because not all countries use cars the same way. People in some countries like smaller cars. These cars take up less space. This is important in busy cities. People in some other countries like big cars.

Where Are Cars Made?

Lots of countries make cars. China and Japan make the most cars. These two countries make millions of cars every year. Chinese companies made over

23 million cars in 2016 alone! Most of those cars were sold in China. Japanese companies made almost 8 million cars in 2016. Japanese cars are sold around the world. Japan is home to Honda and Toyota. Germany is also famous for making cars. Germany is home to companies like Daimler and Volkswagen.

This photo shows a Hyundai factory in Russia.

The United States is known for its cars. General Motors is a large company. Ford is too. Both of those companies were started over one hundred years ago. General Motors was founded in 1908. Ford was founded in 1903. There are important, new car companies in the United States as well. Tesla is a large, new company. It was founded in 2003. It is making electric cars.

Electric cars are made differently than other cars. They are designed to be better for the environment. Electric cars burn less oil to run. That is better for the air.

How Are Cars Made?

Making a car takes a lot of work. It starts with a design. A design is created by an engineer. The design tells the people who build the car what to

DID YOU KNOW?

Today, cars are very quiet. Some people want their cars to make more noise. Companies use speakers to make engine noises and other sounds. This helps people hear cars coming.

Engineers use computer programs to design cars.

include. The design shows how the car will look. It also shows the car's features. Features include screens in the dashboard to help drivers see around the car. They can also include safety features that control locks or windows.

A design is used to make a prototype. This is a car that's built to test the design. The prototype goes through many tests. Any problems found with

Cars are made using robots and other machines.

the prototype need to be fixed. Then, the design can go to production. Production is the step where the car is made. This happens in large factories.

Cars used to be made totally by hand. Today, robotic machines do some of the work. Cars are made on an **assembly line**. An assembly line has different stops where work is done. Robots do work like painting and **welding**. People do work by hand at different stops on the assembly line. For instance, people might put the engine in. Using machines makes it easier and faster to make cars. That also makes cars cheaper.

DID YOU KNOW?

Detroit, Michigan, was once where a lot of cars were made. In the 1930s, just three companies in Detroit made 90 percent of the cars sold in the United States. Today, only about two million cars are made in Detroit a year.

Chapter 3

Selling Cars

More than 80 million cars are bought each year around the world. Almost 20 million are bought in the United States. The average cost of a car in the United States is around $37,000.

A Worldwide Business

Cars are made and sold in many countries around the world. Some cars are made in one country and sold in another. Others are sold in the country where they are made. Bringing cars into a country is called **importing**. Selling cars to another country is called

exporting. It is expensive to sell a car in another country. This means that US-made cars sold in the United States usually cost less. US-made cars sold in China are more expensive. An exported car costs more because of shipping costs.

Millions of people own cars in the United States. Cars became popular in America after World War II. Road networks called highways and interstates made it easier to travel by car. A lot of people moved out of cities. They needed cars to get from place to place. Cars then became more common.

In 2017, over 17 million cars were sold in the United States. Cars are less popular in other parts of the world. In the United Kingdom, only 2.5 million cars were sold in 2017. In Brazil that year, 1.84 million cars were sold. In some countries, cars still cost a lot. That's because not all countries make cars. Some only import them.

In some countries, people travel by public transit. Public transit includes buses and subways. It can also include other ways to get around. Fewer people need cars in those countries.

Shipping Cars

Cars are sent around the world. Shipping cars is not easy. Cars are very heavy. The average car weighs over 4,000 pounds (1,814 kilograms). Because of

DID YOU KNOW?

Basic car features like air conditioning used to cost more than they do now. Today, more expensive features in cars include safety sensors, heated seats, and special radio systems.

their weight, cars have to be shipped carefully.

Cars are usually not driven before someone wants to buy them. That means that a car can't be moved by driving it. Large trailers called auto transports are used to move cars short distances. Auto transports hold more than one car. They attach to trucks. Those trucks take them from place to place.

Some cars are moved on ships so that they can be sold in other countries.

If a car needs to go a long way, it can be moved by train. Trains carry cars long distances. Those cars are then put on auto transports. Trains can cross some borders if countries are close to each other. However, a lot of cars are sold overseas. This means many cars cannot be moved by train.

Ships are used to move cars overseas. Ships can carry a lot of cars. They can also go long distances. Ships pick up cars in one country to take to another. These ships are called car carriers. Cars shipped by sea are sometimes not ready to be sold. Parts like radios are put in cars when they get to where they are going.

Buying and Selling Cars

Cars are advertised by the company that makes them. Cars are sold based on what customers want. Some companies make luxury cars. Luxury cars have special features. These cars cost more. Other cars are sold as family cars. These cars are designed to be very safe. Family cars cost less than luxury cars. Some car companies sell cars that

Luxury car brands include Lamborghini and Bugatti.

are better for the planet. These cars are able to go farther on less gas.

DID YOU KNOW?

In 2017, more than 39 million used cars were sold in America. Used cars are cheaper than new cars. Used cars can be a few years old or very old.

Car buyers can test drive cars at a dealership.

Many cars are sold at businesses called car dealerships. Many dealerships sell one or two types of cars. Some sell new cars. Others sell used cars. This means that someone had owned the car before. Most used cars are cleaned and fixed before being sold.

People who want to buy a car go to a dealership. A car salesperson helps them find the right car. The salesperson also helps them pick out added features and items for their car. That means buying special things that don't usually come with the car. These can be a lot of things, like CD players or floor mats.

Then, the buyer often needs to get a **loan** to pay for the car. The car buyer will also need insurance. That is bought through an insurance company after the car is bought. The buyer can drive their car home that day if it is on the lot (at the dealership) and they have the money to pay for it right away. Some cars have to be shipped to a dealership. Those cars are picked up later.

Chapter 4

Global Connections

Cars are global products. They are made from materials found around the world. They are built in factories in countries like Japan and the United States. They are shipped to every country on Earth. And they have an impact on us all because of the impact they can have on the environment. That's why people around the world are finding new ways to design cars to be safer for drivers, nondrivers, and the planet.

Helping the Planet

People worry about how cars cause pollution. A lot of cars on the road can pollute the air. Countries have passed laws about how cars need to run. These laws say that cars cannot put too many chemicals in the air. The European Union has very strict laws about cars. States in the United States have also passed these kinds of laws. The laws say that cars have to pass a test before they can be sold. Drivers also have to get their cars tested on a schedule. These tests are called emissions tests. They measure how much a car pollutes the air when

DID YOU KNOW?

People can shop for cars on the internet. Buyers can look at cars from far away. This can save money. It also gives people more choices.

it runs. If a car doesn't pass, it cannot be driven. This is to make sure cars are safe for the planet.

Companies are trying to design cars that are better for the planet. Some cars run on electricity. Those cars are very expensive, though. That's why some companies create hybrids. A hybrid is a car that runs on both oil and electricity.

Other companies are testing new kinds of **fuel**. Gasoline can be very bad for the environment. Some cars can run on different fuels. One of these is oil that has been used to cook. It is better for the environment than gasoline.

DID YOU KNOW?

Some companies are designing cars that don't need a driver. These cars are called driverless cars. They are being tested around the world.

Making Cars Safer

People are also worried about car safety. Cars can be very dangerous. They are tested to make sure they're safe. Companies are working to make cars safer too.

Crash test dummies are used to make sure cars are safe.

How can cars be made safer? Cars can be made of stronger materials. This means that a crash won't be as dangerous. Cars can also have safety features. Airbags are one example. Safety features can also be devices that help the driver see around the car. Cameras in the back of the car and screens on the dashboard can show drivers what is behind them as they back up. Sensors can also let drivers know when they are getting close to an object, like another car or a curb.

The Future of Cars

Cars used to be rare. Today, cars are everywhere. People use them in different ways all around the world. The future of

Cities are looking for new ways to limit traffic and keep their roads safe.

cars will be shaped by the impact cars have on our planet. In the future, cars will be safer for everyone and for planet Earth.

Glossary

assembly line A way of making a product that has stations where each step is completed.

body The doors, hood, and other parts of the car that we see.

chassis The frame of a car.

exporting Sending products to another country to be sold.

fuel Something that is burned to make power.

importing Bringing products into a country to be sold.

latex A liquid found in rubber trees that's used to make rubber.

loan Borrowed money that's paid back over time.

welding A way of joining metal.

Find Out More

Books

Machajewski, Sarah. *All About Cars*. Let's Find Out!
New York, NY: Rosen Publishing, 2017.

West, David. *Cars*. Inside Machines. New York, NY:
Rosen Publishing, 2018.

Websites

DK Find Out! History of Cars

*https://www.dkfindout.com/us/
transportation/history-cars*

This website shows the history of cars.

How a Car Is Made: Parts 1–6

https://youtu.be/PSLroLJEI9M

Watch this video for a fun look at how a car is made.

Index

About the Author

Bridey Heing is an author who writes about books, history, and current events. Her other books include *How Is Software Made and Sold?* Heing lives in Washington, DC. She likes to read, hike, and go to museums.